בְּרֵאשִׁית

IN THE
BEGINNING

בְּרֵאשִׁית

IN THE
BEGINNING

Adapted by
Alison Greengard

Illustrated by
Carol Racklin-Siegel

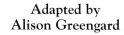

THE STORY OF CREATION
EXCERPTED FROM GENESIS

EKS Publishing Co., Albany, California

Adapted by
Alison Greengard

Illustrated by
Carol Racklin-Siegel

Editor
Jessica Goldstein

Book Design
Irene Imfeld

EKS Publishing Co.
P.O. Box 9750
Berkeley, CA 94709-0750
e-mail: EKS@wenet.net
Phone (510) 558-9200 Fax (510) 558-9255

First Printing, September 2000
ISBN 0-939144-34-4

Introduction

In *The Beginning* introduces young readers to the story of Creation in Genesis. The Hebrew is excerpted from the first two chapters of the Bible, and although we omitted words to keep the language simple, we did not change or add any text. Each page offers a meaningful—but not always literal—translation. For readers studying Hebrew, we have included a literal translation at the end of the story. A glossary at the back of the book gives the meaning and pronunciation of each word in *In The Beginning*. The glossary lists words exactly as they appear in the story. We hope that readers of all ages will enjoy this retelling of Creation and come to love and appreciate the language and beauty of the Hebrew Bible.

To my children, Rachel and David, who
always let me know there are new and
different ways to do things.
—Alison

To my mother, Mary Racklin, who
inspired me to make art.
—Carol

בְּרֵאשִׁית
IN THE
BEGINNING

בְּרֵאשִׁית בָּרָא אֱלֹהִים אֵת הַשָּׁמַיִם וְאֵת הָאָרֶץ.
וַיֹּאמֶר אֱלֹהִים יְהִי אוֹר. וַיְהִי אוֹר.
וַיִּקְרָא אֱלֹהִים לָאוֹר יוֹם וְלַחשֶׁךְ קָרָא לָיְלָה.
וַיְהִי עֶרֶב וַיְהִי בֹקֶר יוֹם אֶחָד.

In the beginning, when God was creating the heaven
and the earth, God said, "Let there be light!"
And there was light. God called the light Day.
The darkness God called Night. It was evening and
it was morning, the first day.

וַיֹּאמֶר אֱלֹהִים יְהִי רָקִיעַ בְּתוֹךְ הַמָּיִם.
וַיִּקְרָא אֱלֹהִים לָרָקִיעַ שָׁמָיִם.
וַיְהִי עֶרֶב וַיְהִי בֹקֶר יוֹם שֵׁנִי.

God said, "Let there be a space in the
middle of the water." God called the space Sky.
It was evening and it was morning,
the second day.

וַיֹּאמֶר אֱלֹהִים יִקָּווּ הַמַּיִם מִתַּחַת הַשָּׁמַיִם אֶל
מָקוֹם אֶחָד וְתֵרָאֶה הַיַּבָּשָׁה. וַיְהִי כֵן. וַיִּקְרָא
אֱלֹהִים לַיַּבָּשָׁה אֶרֶץ וּלְמִקְוֵה הַמַּיִם קָרָא יַמִּים.
וַיַּרְא אֱלֹהִים כִּי טוֹב.

God said, "Let the waters under the sky be collected
in one place, and let the dry land appear."
It was so. God called the dry land Earth,
and the water God called Seas.
God saw that it was good.

וַיֹּאמֶר אֱלֹהִים תַּדְשֵׁא הָאָרֶץ דֶּשֶׁא עֵשֶׂב.
וַיְהִי כֵן. וַיַּרְא אֱלֹהִים כִּי טוֹב.
וַיְהִי עֶרֶב וַיְהִי בֹקֶר יוֹם שְׁלִישִׁי.

God said, "Let the earth sprout plants."
It was so, and God saw that it was good.
It was evening and it was morning,
the third day.

וַיֹּאמֶר אֱלֹהִים יְהִי מְאֹרֹת בִּרְקִיעַ הַשָּׁמַיִם.
וַיְהִי כֵן. וַיַּעַשׂ אֱלֹהִים אֶת הַמְּאֹרֹת הַגְּדֹל
לְמֶמְשֶׁלֶת הַיּוֹם וְאֶת הַמָּאוֹר הַקָּטֹן לְמֶמְשֶׁלֶת
הַלַּיְלָה וְאֶת הַכּוֹכָבִים. וַיַּרְא אֱלֹהִים כִּי טוֹב.
וַיְהִי עֶרֶב וַיְהִי בֹקֶר יוֹם רְבִיעִי.

God said, "Let there be lights in the sky!"
It was so. God made the bigger light to rule the day,
the smaller light to rule the night, and the stars.
God saw that it was good. It was evening and
it was morning, the fourth day.

וַיֹּאמֶר אֱלֹהִים יִשְׁרְצוּ הַמַּיִם שֶׁרֶץ
נֶפֶשׁ חַיָּה וְעוֹף יְעוֹפֵף עַל הָאָרֶץ.
וַיַּרְא אֱלֹהִים כִּי טוֹב. וַיְבָרֶךְ אֹתָם
אֱלֹהִים. וַיְהִי עֶרֶב וַיְהִי בֹקֶר יוֹם חֲמִישִׁי.

God said, "Let the waters be filled with fish,
and let birds fly above the earth."
God saw that it was good. God blessed them.
It was evening and it was morning,
the fifth day.

וַיֹּאמֶר אֱלֹהִים תּוֹצֵא הָאָרֶץ נֶפֶשׁ חַיָּה. וַיְהִי כֵן.
וַיַּרְא אֱלֹהִים כִּי טוֹב. וַיִּבְרָא אֱלֹהִים אֶת
הָאָדָם בְּצַלְמוֹ. זָכָר וּנְקֵבָה. וַיְבָרֶךְ אֹתָם אֱלֹהִים.
וַיַּרְא אֱלֹהִים אֶת כָּל אֲשֶׁר עָשָׂה וְהִנֵּה טוֹב מְאֹד.
וַיְהִי עֶרֶב וַיְהִי בֹקֶר יוֹם הַשִּׁשִּׁי.

God said, "Let there be animals on the earth."
It was so, and God saw that it was good.
God created people in God's image. Male and female,
God created them. God blessed them. God saw all
that had been made, and indeed, it was very good.
It was evening and it was morning, the sixth day.

וַיְכֻלּוּ הַשָּׁמַיִם וְהָאָרֶץ וְכָל צְבָאָם.
וַיְכַל אֱלֹהִים בַּיּוֹם הַשְּׁבִיעִי
מְלַאכְתּוֹ אֲשֶׁר עָשָׂה וַיִּשְׁבֹּת. וַיְבָרֶךְ
אֱלֹהִים אֶת יוֹם הַשְּׁבִיעִי וַיְקַדֵּשׁ אֹתוֹ.

The sky and the earth and all their parts
were completed. On the seventh day,
God finished all the work of creation and rested.
God blessed the seventh day
and made it holy.

In the beginning, God created the heavens and the earth. And God said, "Let there be light." And there was light. God called the light "day," and the darkness he called "night." And it was evening and it was morning, a first day.

Then God said, "Let there be a dome in the middle of the water." And God called the dome "sky." And it was evening and it was morning, a second day.

God said, "Let the water under the sky be gathered together into one place, and let the dry land appear." And it was so. And God called the dry land "earth," and the gathered water he called "seas."

God said, "Let the earth sprout vegetation." It was so, and God saw that it was good. It was evening and it was morning, a third day.

God said, "Let there be lights in the dome of the sky." And it was so. God made the greater light to rule the day, and the lesser light to rule the night, and the stars. God saw that it was good. And it was evening and it was morning, a fourth day.

God said, "Let the waters bring forth swarms of living creatures, and let birds fly above the earth." God saw that it was good, and God blessed them. And it was evening and it was morning, a fifth day.

God said, "Let the earth bring forth living creatures." It was so, and God saw that it was good. God created man in his image; male and female he created them. And God blessed them. God saw all that he had created, and indeed, it was very good. And it was evening and it was morning, a sixth day.

The sky and the earth were finished, and all their array. On the seventh day God finished all the work that he had done and rested. And God blessed the seventh day, and he sanctified it.

Glossary

א

א	**a**-lef	one
אוֹר	**or**	light
אֶחָד	e-**chad**	one/first
אֶל	**el**	to/toward
אֱלֹהִים	e-lo-**heem**	God
אֶרֶץ	**e**-rets	earth
אֲשֶׁר	a-**sher**	that/which
אֵת	**ayt**	not translatable
אֶת	**et**	not translatable
אֹתוֹ	o-**to**	it
אֹתָם	o-**tam**	them

ב

ב	**bayt**	two
בַּיּוֹם	ba-**yom**	on the day
בְּצַלְמוֹ	b-tsal-**mo**	in his (God's) image
בֹקֶר	**vo**-ker	morning
בָּרָא	ba-**ra**	created
בִּרְקִיעַ	beer-**kee**-a	in the space of/in the dome of
בְּרֵאשִׁית	b-ray-**sheet**	in the beginning
בְּתוֹךְ	b-**toch**	in the middle of

20

ג

| ג | **g**-mel | three |

ד

| ד | **da**-let | four |
| דֶּשֶׁא | **de**-she | plants/vegetation |

ה

ה	**hay**	five
הָאָדָם	ha-a-**dam**	the man/people
הָאָרֶץ	ha-**a**-rets	the earth
הַגָּדוֹל	ha-ga-**dol**	bigger
הַיַּבָּשָׁה	ha-ya-ba-**sha**	the dry land
הַיּוֹם	hay-**yom**	the day
הַכּוֹכָבִים	ha-ko-cha-**veem**	the stars
הַלַּיְלָה	ha-**lai**-la	the night
הַמָּאוֹר	ha-ma-**or**	the light
הַמַּיִם	ha-**ma**-yeem	the water
הַקָּטֹן	ha-ka-**ton**	smaller
הַשְּׁבִיעִי	hash-vee-**ee**	seventh
הַשָּׁמַיִם	ha-sha-**ma**-yeem	the heaven
הַשִּׁשִּׁי	ha-shee-**shee**	sixth

ו

ו	vav	six
וְאֵת	v-**ayt**	and
וְאֶת	v-**et**	and
וְהָאָרֶץ	v-ha-**a**-rets	and the earth
וְהִנֵּה	v-heen-**nay**	and look/and see
וַיֹּאמֶר	vay-yo-**mer**	and he (God) said
וַיִּבְרָא	vay-yeev-**ra**	and he (God) created
וַיְבָרֶךְ	vay-va-**rech**	and he (God) blessed
וַיְהִי	va-y-**hee**	and there was
וַיְכַל	vay-**chal**	and he (God) finished
וַיְכֻלּוּ	vay-choo-**loo**	were finished
וַיַּעַשׂ	vay-ya-**as**	and he (God) made
וַיְקַדֵּשׁ	vay-ka-**desh**	and he (God) made holy
וַיִּקְרָא	vay-yeek-**ra**	and he (God) called
וַיַּרְא	vay-**yar**	and he (God) saw
וַיִּשְׁבֹּת	vay-yeesh-**bot**	and he (God) rested
וְלַחֹשֶׁךְ	v-la-**cho**-shech	and the darkness
וְכָל	v-**chol**	and all of
וּלְמִקְוֵה	ul-meek-**vay**	gathered
וּנְקֵבָה	oon-kay-**va**	and female

22

אבגדהוזחטיכלמנסעפצקרשת

ו

| וָעוֹף | v-**of** | and birds |
| וְתֵרָאֶה | v-tay-ra-**e** | and let appear |

ז

| זָכָר | za-**char** | male |

ח

| חַיָּה | chay-**ya** | living |
| חֲמִישִׁי | cha-mee-**shee** | fifth |

ט

| טוֹב | **tov** | good, it was good |

י

יְהִי	y-**hee**	let there be
יוֹם	**yom**	day
יַמִּים	yam-**meem**	seas
יְעוֹפֵף	y-o-**fayf**	let fly
יִקָּווּ	yeek-ka-**voo**	be collected/be gathered
יִשְׁרְצוּ	yeesh-r-**tsoo**	be filled/let bring forth

כ

כִּי	kee	that
כִּי טוֹב	kee tov	that it was good
כָּל	kol	all
כֵּן	chayn	so

ל

לָאוֹר	la-**or**	the light
לַיַּבָּשָׁה	la-ya-ba-**sha**	the dry land
לַיְלָה	**lai**-la	night
לְמֶמְשֶׁלֶת	l-mem-**she**-let	to rule
לָרָקִיעַ	la-ra-**kee**-a	the space/the dome

מ

מְאֹד	m-**od**	very
מְאֹרֹת	m-o-**rot**	lights
מְלַאכְתּוֹ	m-lach-**to**	his work
מָקוֹם	ma-**kom**	place
מִתַּחַת	meet-**ta**-chat	under

נ

נֶפֶשׁ	**ne**-fesh	life/living being
נֶפֶשׁ חַיָּה	**ne**-fesh chay-**ya**	living being(s)/creature(s)

א ב ג ד ה ו ז ח ט י כ ל מ נ ס ע פ צ ק ר ש ת

ע

עַל	**al**	above
עֶרֶב	**e**-rev	evening
עֵשֶׂב	ay-**sev**	plants, grass
עָשָׂה	a-**sa**	he (God) had done

צ

צְבָאָם	ts-va-**am**	their parts/their array

ק

קָרָא	ka-**ra**	he (God) called

ר

רְבִיעִי	r-vee-**ee**	fourth
רָקִיעַ	ra-**kee**-a	space/dome

ש

שְׁלִישִׁי	sh-lee-**shee**	third
שָׁמַיִם	sha-**ma**-yeem	heaven/heavens
שֵׁנִי	shay-**nee**	second
שֶׁרֶץ	**she**-rets	swarm of

ת

תַּדְשֵׁא	tad-**shay**	let sprout
תּוֹצֵא	to-**tsay**	let bring forth

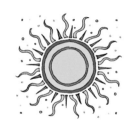